The Winner's Mind

Strengthening Mental Skills in Athletes

Lynda Lahman, MA

ISBN-13: 978-1500542672
ISBN-10: 1500542679
LCCN: 2014913034

To Terry, for your unfailing support of all I do

PROLOGUE

I remember my first pair of tennis shoes: Converse high tops, hand-me-downs from my older brother. From that moment on, dolls were ignored and I lived outside. Running, chasing, building forts, shooting pellet guns, and playing every sport offered before and after school. Kickball and flag football were my favorites, challenging me to run fast, play hard, and work with my teammates to achieve success. I loved horses, but my mother was allergic to them and money was tight, so my lessons were few and far between; my passion was limited to a collection of early Breyer horses that unfortunately, I gave away sometime in adolescence.

Transitioning to junior high, I was shocked to discover it was no longer cool to want to aggressively pursue athletics. It wasn't feminine and there were no leagues or teams that allowed girls to play with the boys. A brief interlude in a private school encouraged participation in track and field, which was quickly followed by a return to public school and physical education classes that discouraged sweating. Title IX was signed into law the year I graduated high school, too late for me to benefit from its purpose of providing equality for girls in sports.

I turned my competitiveness and athleticism to the outdoors. I began hiking and backpacking, gaining confidence in my ability to cover long distances, work with limited supplies, and endure hardships while enjoying camaraderie with fellow hikers and the beauty of nature.

Always passionate about sports, in my early thirties I returned to playing. Picking up a tennis racket felt like coming home, and ten years later I started competing. I realized I had more to learn than the mechanics, however. I had to learn how to compete effectively, how to lose without becoming frustrated, and how to focus my energy and attention despite both internal and external distractions.

Drawing on my years of experience as a therapist, and particularly as a mindfulness-based clinician, I soon saw the benefits of applying the skills I used in my practice to my personal sports endeavors. Additional training in sports psychology plus life and wellness coaching coalesced in my head, and the path of my work became clear.

The world of competitive long distance motorcycling took my skills to a new level. My tennis competitions required quick reactive skills and focus, while riding required endurance, both physically and mentally. As part of my training for long distances, I began running half marathons, learning more about myself and my ability to achieve success over an extended period of time despite hunger, exhaustion, and discouragement.

Leaving my psychotherapy practice to focus exclusively on mental skills coaching, I now help athletes of all levels find their way to success. Having gone through ups and downs on my own personal journey I understand the steps necessary to achieve the accomplishments others seek. The steps are teachable, and whether it's completing a first 5K walk/run, improving focus in golf, competing in a Grand Prix riding event, or the challenge of obtaining a personal best in an Ironman, my passion is helping athletes learn how to be their best. Helping athletes move beyond mental barriers to become mental giants is my goal. This book introduces you to some of the mental skills that can help you reach your own dreams.

My work follows the ACT model. ACT stands for Acceptance and Commitment Therapy. It is a mindfulness-based approach designed to help you accept, rather than fight, with uncomfortable thoughts and feelings while moving toward things you value. There are six main components of this approach, which I have categorized for the purposes of this book as Values and Vision, The Stories We Tell, The Chattering Mind, Being Comfortable With The Uncomfortable, Being Present, When It All Falls Apart, and Putting It All Together. Each component interweaves with the rest, and while I have presented them in a particular sequence, you may read the chapters in whichever order you choose.

I encourage you to share your experiences with your coach, trainer, or pro. These exercises are designed to complement your personal or team training program, and should be practiced with the same attention, effort, and regularity you apply to your physical workouts. As with any skill, repeated practice builds confidence and competence.

CONTENTS

A NOTE BEFORE BEGINNING

Imagine for a moment you are watching your favorite athlete give a flawless performance. Clearly he or she is 'in the zone' and it is a thing of beauty to behold. At first, you are completely mesmerized by the fluidity of movement, the gracefulness of the action, the intensity of the focus. The world exists only in that moment.

Then slowly you notice your mind beginning to come alive.

~ *I'll never be that good.*

~ *My body can't do what hers is doing.*

~ *He's better than I am because he must have all the money in the world to buy the best horse and spend all day practicing.*

~ *I used to be that good before my accident. Now I'm freaked out and afraid of things that never scared me before.*

Soon the performance has faded and the chatter takes over. The simple act of observing transitioned to one of critiquing and judging. Later in the book we'll look at what to do with the chatter, but for now I want to point out the concept of the 'observing self,' the part of our mind that doesn't think—it merely observes.

While you were fully engaged in the performance, you were simply observing. You weren't thinking, you were only noticing. Once the chatter started, your brain moved away from observer and into thinker. Sometimes, your observing self comes back online and you realize what just occurred. Other times it happens so quickly you aren't even aware that your observer self has been hijacked.

The exercises in this book will ask you to 'notice' and to 'notice what shows up for you.' It is from this space of observer that I am asking you to notice. Noticing without filters, without judgment, without critique.

There is no need to silence the judgments, simply notice them. There is no need to control where your brain or emotions take you, simply notice where they go. Whatever comes up is information, and that information will be useful in each of the exercises. Curiosity is the key. Ask your mind to be curious, to notice, and to learn.

CHAPTER 1

INTRODUCTION

~ *I purchased a bombproof horse. He won't spook at anything; he's sweet and predictable. But I'm still scared to ride when the wind blows or someone else is in the arena with a frisky horse. I'm still afraid something will happen despite everything I've done to make it safe.*

~ *I've paid thousands for lessons to improve my game, and I still choke in tournaments. My pro says I have all the skills to win, but I lack confidence. I think if I keep taking lessons I'll get to the point where I believe in myself enough to finally win.*

~ *My coach tells me to concentrate when I'm about to start down the slope, so I tell myself to 'concentrate.' I even yell it to myself before I take off, but nothing seems to work.*

~ *I love running marathons but I get so anxious before a race. Believe it or not, I throw up almost every time I'm in a competitive situation. I don't throw up when I'm training. I can't seem to make myself calm down. I feel like an idiot and keep telling myself to stop. I've varied how I eat, my pacing, my self-talk; nothing seems to work. I'm beginning to dread my next race.*

~ *Every sport psychology self-help book tells me to visualize success. I just keep screwing up, and usually in really stupid ways despite believing I'm capable of winning. If I can only figure out how to translate the visualizations into reality I'd be fine.*

~ If I just try harder I can get my fear of crashing under control. I start to get better and then I read about an accident and I'm right back where I started. Maybe I should just quit and sell my bike.

~ I used to ride without a care. Now that I have kids, I'm terrified of getting hurt. What's wrong with me? Where did that fearless younger me go?

Most athletes have been trained to work hard, and most have read about positive self-talk. Coaches and trainers stress focusing and staying calm, staying 'in the zone.' Yet few coaches know how to teach those skills. As a result, athletes assume they should know how to focus, how to let go of fears, how to stay calm, and how to be in the moment.

Think about your own journey. Has a coach, trainer, parent, or teammate suggested you 'get it together' or 'stop being so timid, just go for it?' Wanting to do better, have you looked for more instruction; the magic solution of the perfect horse, equipment, or team; the right combination of practice and self-talk to finally succeed? Are you beating yourself up because your life situation has changed and you aren't as daring as you once were? Do you have an amazing outing one time, then blow it the next?

Certainly some of the things you have tried have resulted in improved performance. But it is often the case that one more self-help book, one more lesson with the pro, or one more attempt to regain focus by yelling at yourself to try harder has yet to create a better outcome. Perhaps it is time to try a different approach.

Exercise 1: What You've Already Tried

Make a list of all the things you've done to alleviate your fears, stop negative thoughts, eliminate uncomfortable feelings, or help you improve your mental focus.

Which things that you tried resulted in changing the results, whether reducing your fear or improving your performance?

Which things that you tried resulted in keeping things the same, or perhaps even making them worse?

~

Exercise 2: Creative Helplessness

Make a list of things you have yet to try, but are thinking about doing.

Look back at your list in Exercise 1, and compare the two. Is there anything substantially different between the two lists?

How much have you invested in trying to change things only to have them remain the same? Realistically, will doing more of the same result in a different outcome?

~

Take a moment and answer the following questions:

Are you willing to let go of getting rid of your fear and accept that it may always be there?

Are you willing to practice smarter, not just harder?

Are you willing to invest time, money, and energy in learning new skills that will help your mental game and lead to success in many areas of your life... not just sports?

Hopefully, you answered yes to all of the above.

CHAPTER 2

VALUES AND VISION

My father introduced me to the game of tennis when I was in elementary school. He'd seen young prodigies and their successes, and got it into his head that I could be a brilliant player as well. I had nice strokes, good speed, and enjoyed hitting the ball. My parents, divorced when I was one, often lived on separate coasts, so my tennis lessons took place when my dad was in town, too infrequently to make much difference in my life. As a result, nothing came of my early promise, and although I played for a time in junior high, I didn't really become enthusiastic about the game until I was approaching my forties.

For years I wondered what might have happened had my dad lived closer. My guess is it would have been a disaster. I loved playing all sports and being athletic, but I doubt I had the focus, drive, and passion to settle on a single sport and dedicate myself to a life of practice, competitions, and winning. It was my father's dream of glory, not mine.

When I picked up the racket as an adult, the dream was mine, the willingness to work to improve my game was mine, and the dedication to practice came from within me.

The question my father never asked was 'Why are you playing?' followed by, 'Who are you playing for?' He wasn't able separate his interests from mine; he wasn't curious to know if I had a deeper motivation for participating in tennis at any level. Why is that important?

If my father had lived closer, I know he'd have encouraged me to play tennis. He would have had me out practicing and taking me to lessons. He'd share his knowledge of the game with me, giving me tips and telling me about other players and their successes. I might have experienced our time together initially as fun and supportive. But I know over time I would have felt pressure to achieve, to improve, and to win. That pressure would not have come from within, but from my desire to see myself as my father saw me: a champion. It would have also come from a subtler but equally compelling need to make him happy. He wanted to be a success himself, and had not achieved it in the many endeavors he had pursued. He wanted to live through any glory I might achieve, and as a loving, caring daughter, I would have done anything for him to have his dream.

But his dream wasn't mine, and thankfully, I wasn't put in the position of having to fulfill his. I was free to explore my own pursuits and ambitions. I was allowed to decide for myself where my passions lay, and in the process learn what I was willing to do to achieve my own success. I want to you to discover the same for yourself.

~

A critical component of successful performance is to understand the real reasons for participating in the activity. Too often, the reasons are external: wanting approval from someone, trying to live up to another's expectations, or proving one's self worth. While these may be initially motivating, it is ultimately more satisfying and sustaining to connect with a personally held passion regarding performance. In that case, the activity nurtures a core part of oneself and is therefore a reward in itself, no matter the outcome of a specific event.

Do you know why you compete? Why you choose to ride hunter/jumper instead of dressage? What is motivating you to attempt an Ironman rather than stick with another marathon? Why you workout regularly at the gym or take yoga? Is it for fitness, to lose weight, or to bring home a trophy?

In the following exercises, you are going to be asked to dig a little deeper, to figure out what is behind those reasons in search of something even more important: a value. Values, unlike goals, are tied to a deeper sense of purpose, of meaning. By understanding the values behind what we do, we can more deeply commit to honoring them and recognize the motivating power they provide.

Read through each exercise first to understand what you are being asked to do, and then take as long as you need to complete each one. Have a paper and pen nearby so you can write your answers.

Exercise 3: Discovering What Matters

Find a comfortable place to sit, and take a few moments to become still by focusing on your breathing, bringing your attention back to your breath when your mind wanders. Next, bring your attention to your chosen activity. Picture yourself getting ready for your activity, perhaps getting dressed in a particular set of clothes and heading to the location where you will participate. It might be in your home, your back yard, a local park, the barn, a fitness center, or perhaps your local golf course; whatever comes to mind for you.

Picture the entire scene: the colors, the sights, the sounds, the feel of the air on your skin. Now begin moving, taking your first steps, warming up, and just notice how your body feels. Simply notice. Without judging them, notice any thoughts that drift through your mind. Allow them to pass through as if they came in one side of your head and flowed out the other as you bring your attention back to your imagery. Take a few moments to continue your activity, as you move from warming up into full participation, simply noticing your body, the sensations you experience, and your thoughts as they drift through your mind.

~ I imagined playing tennis on a Saturday morning with three of my friends. We chatted as we got our rackets out and decided our plan for the morning. We shared some stories about our families, and laughed about a story one of the women told. We went out on the court and started with a warm-up before practicing some drills we learned in our lesson earlier in the week. Finally, we finished with a set. I noticed I became more competitive once we started our drills, and it intensified when we played the set. I could hear a voice in my head yelling at me when my serve went wide. I felt great when I hit an overhead at my opponent and she couldn't get to it. I got frustrated with my partner when she missed a shot in the final game. I didn't say anything but I

noticed I hesitated a moment too long to want to shake everyone's hand at the net. Sometimes I hate that I care so much about winning.

Now imagine that someone approaches you and tells you must stop; you can no longer do this activity. Notice your immediate reaction. It doesn't need to make sense to you, simply notice.

~ *I immediately thought of the other women I play with. I have a lot of fun with most of them, and we usually go out to coffee after we play. I imagined missing out on that, and it felt terrible. I then thought about working in the drills and lessons, and pushing myself to get better. I really like challenging myself. I thought about other sports, and it's the same thing: being active, being with others, and pushing myself.*

What happened when your activity was taken away?

What was the activity providing for you? What about that was important for you?

If it you pictured winning a medal, what would it mean for you? How might that be important?

If it's being active, why is that important for you?

If it's losing weight, what will that bring you? What about that would be important?

Take a moment and let your mind wander to a deeper place: what else shows up?

Continue with this exploration, turning each answer over to see what might lie beneath it, continuing down this path to see at each turn what shows up as being essential to you. Continue asking 'and what would be important about that' until you come to something that feels right, something that feels the most important to you.

Bring your attention back to the activity itself. Imagine participating with the knowledge of why it is so important to you. See yourself embracing mindfully the value you have tapped into as you once again imagine your chosen activity. Notice your body, your physical sensations, and your thoughts as they drift through your mind.

What did you discover? Is this a new awareness or something you have always known? Did it surprise you or confirm your convictions? Not everyone comes up with a positive value. Occasionally what is learned is that the reasons for doing something are only to gain approval or fill an emptiness. If that is what you experienced, this can be an opportunity to explore more deeply why that is important to you, what is it you really want, and if you were to get it, what it would mean. For example, if what came up is 'to impress others' what would happen if you did impress them? Would you be loved? And what would be important about that? Would you feel a greater acceptance of yourself? Then what if the value you hold is to feel good about yourself? Is there a way you can participate in your activity to honor that value in and of itself?

Exercise 4: Exploring Sport Specific Values

Following is a list of some of the reasons why people participate in sports. Choose ten from the list, and put them in order of importance. Add any reasons you don't find listed.

A sense of accomplishment

Adventure/excitement

Analyze performance

Be a good sport

Become physically fit

Belong to a group

Challenge

Clear tasks

Coach others

Competition

Connect with animals

Connect with nature

Dare to dream

Develop skills

Enjoyment

Execute a plan

Feel competent

Freedom

Gain confidence

Interact with teammates

Learn to trust my teammates

Love of the sport

Measure progress

Motivation to eat well

Motivation to care for my body

Prestige

Push my limits

Reduce stress

Take a moment and reflect on your list. What stands out? What feels most important to you? Did the same things show up on this list that stood out in the first exercise, or were there some new ones?

The next step is to formulate a personal vision statement: a summary of your philosophy, why you engage in any activity, and what you are hoping to accomplish, all based on your core values. The purpose is to help you understand who you are and who you want to be as you participate. This vision statement will become the cornerstone of your success.

Exercise 5: What's Your Vision?

Think about the following questions to help develop your personal vision statement. Take your time to answer each one as fully as possible.

Who do you want to be as an athlete?

What is at the core of why you participate?

If you had to stop, what would you miss the most?

How do you want to view yourself?

How do you want to be described by others?

What does it mean to you to be an excellent athlete?

What does it mean to you to be a good teammate?

What kind of teammate do you want to be?

Why are sports important to you?

Do you value hard work?

Prestige?

Enjoyment?

Effort?

Learning new skills?

Challenging yourself?

Helping others learn?

Developing your skills?

What would you like to do more of?

How important is it to you that you participate for others?

How important is it to you that you participate for yourself?

After considering the above questions, combine your answers with any additional thoughts or discoveries from the previous exercises and begin writing a personal vision statement that accurately reflects your philosophy: what you want to stand for no matter what sport you are participating in.

~ I want to fully participate in my life, not watch from the sidelines. I want to push myself to see what I am capable of while being a good teammate to others. I want to demonstrate leadership and kindness, being a good example in all that I do. Winning reflects hard work and losing challenges me to dig deeper and learn more about how to be better. When I look back at my life in sports, I want to know I didn't avoid the hard work, and that if I chose to stop doing something it was because doing so aligned with my values.

~ Connection with my horse is at the core of everything I do. Developing a partnership, learning to work and grow together are the most important aspects of riding. I love the adrenaline rush of jumping. Competitions challenge me to grow, give me something to strive for, and introduce me to others who share my passion.

~ I run for the sheer joy of it. I want to run as long as I am alive, and I am willing to take the long view so I can stay fit. I value the alone time on long runs, a time for reflection and meditation, to clear my head and remember what is important in my life. I value encouraging others to share in my passion, and I want to take the time to volunteer teaching children to become lifelong runners.

~ I want to keep growing, to try new things, to push my envelope. I want to experience life fully, without fear of failing and with a joy in living. I want to come skidding in at the end, knowing I pushed myself to be my best.

~ I am a serious competitor. I want to work hard and bring my best every time I play, whether in practice or a match. Competing helps me keep my life in balance. Having concrete goals gives me something to aspire to, whether or not I achieve them; the process of working toward them makes me a better person and helps me focus in all the other aspects of my life.

Exercise 6: Using Your Vision Statement

Now that you have written your personal statement, spend a few moments visualizing what it means to you. Focus on breathing in the values as you say the words gently to yourself. With each reading, feel it moving deeper into your body, into your consciousness. When you feel you have a clear sense of connection with your vision, continue with this exercise.

Sit quietly and imagine yourself participating in your chosen activity, with your statement of values clearly in your mind. If your mind wanders, as minds often do, simply come back to the words and your breath.

Now, imagine a time when you struggled while participating in your activity, when you felt discouraged, tired, frustrated, bored; whatever your struggle might be. A time when maybe you felt like quitting or getting angry and lashing out. Visualize such a time as vividly as you can, and notice what thoughts, feelings, and sensations come up. Intensify those for a moment, and simply notice.

Now, bring your personal statement to mind and breathe. With each breath, simply focus on your stated values, breathe, and notice. Take a few moments to breathe in your values and notice what you are experiencing.

After a few moments, open your eyes and write down your observations.

~

Was this exercise helpful for you? Can you imagine this being useful while you are participating in your activity and things begin to become challenging? Rather than arguing with yourself or 'pumping yourself up,' what might it be like to simply breathe in your values? To quietly remind yourself of your personal philosophy? To return to what is essential and important to you?

Practice reflecting on your vision statement and values before you engage in your activity. Take a few minutes in the car before you go into the gym, sit on a bench in the barn before grooming your horse, or give yourself extra time to center yourself before a competition. Reflect again on your philosophy as you are heading back home: did you act in accordance with your values today? When you found yourself acting in conflict with them were you able to notice and reconnect with them? Did it change your behavior or your experience in any way? Was it helpful?

Keep a notebook or log with your observations. Notice what works best for you, and see if being mindful of what is helpful has an impact on your performance and your enjoyment of your activity.

CHAPTER 3

THE STORIES WE TELL

~ *I fell off my horse ten years ago, and broke my back. I was in the arena alone and had to crawl across the ground to reach the phone. I had asked the horse to canter; when he lurched forward awkwardly I lost my balance and I've been afraid something like that might happen again. Since then I've chosen mellow, bombproof horses, to help relieve my anxiety. When it's windy outside I dread getting on any horse, afraid something might spook them and I'll fall.*

~ *I want to train for a triathlon but I freak out at the thought of swimming with a group. When I was ten I tried sitting on a surfboard and got knocked over by a small wave. I was spun around underwater and couldn't figure out which way was up. I was terrified I would drown. Luckily, I hit the sand on the bottom and was able to push myself up to the surface before I ran out of air. When I was in my early thirties I went to the lake with some friends and we swam out a ways from the shore. The water was murky and I kept feeling something against my feet, and it creeped me out. I kept imagining something was trying to grab me and pull me under.*

~ *I've never been good at running. I grew up where it was smoggy, and every time we had to run in PE I could barely breathe. Our teacher made us run laps, and I was always in trouble for needing to walk. If I tried running faster, I'd be gasping for air. I felt like an idiot in front of my friends.*

~ *I can play really well when I'm practicing, but I lose it in matches. I start out well, but if I mess up one hole I can't recover. I get frustrated and keep telling myself to calm down and get it together, but it just doesn't work. Once I start down that path it's all over.*

~ My first competition was awesome. I didn't know what to expect, and I nailed it. I remember the feeling of being handed the blue ribbon and the look on my parents' faces. They were so proud of me! The next few times I competed were fun, but then I began to feel a pressure to do well. I kept looking for my trainer, worried he would be disappointed if I failed to place. I began telling myself I had to keep winning; it wasn't okay to fail. It was easier when no one expected anything from me.

~ I was an incredible rider as a junior. I was fearless and loved riding the challenging horses. I loved the adrenaline rush and the thrill of competing. Now I'm hesitant when my horse acts up, trying to calm us both down instead of figuring out how to use his energy to make us better. There wasn't a particular event that occurred; I just noticed it's been getting worse since I had children.

Everyone has stories of successes and failures. Sometimes the stories generate laughs, sometimes empathy, occasionally shock, and often knowing nods: *'Yes, I've been there, done that.'* But stories may also unknowingly reinforce beliefs about yourself that might be contributing to keeping you stuck.

Exercise 7: The Stories You Tell Others

Take a moment to think about a few of the stories you tell repeatedly. For this exercise, focus on those related to your sport. Write them down in as much detail as you do when you are sharing them with others.

~ *My first time on a motorcycle was in the new riders' class. The bike was small and easy to maneuver. I felt like a rock star when I passed the driver's test. I was really excited when I went shopping for my first bike. I liked one a bit bigger than the one we used in class, and it was similar in style so I thought it'd be good to start with. My friend suggested I get a slightly larger bike, knowing I'd quickly outgrow the one I'd picked. I really wanted the smaller one, but I overruled my gut feeling and went with his recommendation. He was a much better rider so he must know more than I did.*

When the bike was moving I had no trouble handling it, but at low speeds and stops I struggled. It was too tall, too heavy, and just too much for me. Several times I fell, and I began to lose confidence and got scared. I started to avoid riding, finding excuses to cover my embarrassment. My fear of falling slowly overtook my desire to ride on my own. I hated myself for being a wimp, and I hated my friend for pushing me into buying the wrong bike. Maybe I wasn't really meant to ride solo. Finally, I quit altogether; convincing myself I preferred being a passenger.

~

Now, go back through your stories, and answer the following:

What is the primary emotion you feel when you tell this story?

What are your thoughts about yourself when you tell this story?

Does this story in some way help you perform better?

Is it a story of strength that you find useful?

Does this story in some way diminish how you see yourself as a performer?

Is this a story with judgments and criticisms that are hurtful or frightening?

Exercise 8: Just The Facts, Please

Choose one of your stories from the previous exercise. Write it again, but this time tell only the objective facts, leaving aside any of the emotions and judgments you usually include when you tell it.

~ *My first time on a motorcycle was in the new riders' class. We rode on small bikes. I went shopping for a new bike. I bought a bigger bike. I fell several times at stops. I decided to stop riding my own bike, and continued riding as a passenger.*

What, if anything, do you notice is different in this version?

What might be helpful in telling the story in this manner?

Exercise 9: Telling A New Story

Take the facts from the story in Exercise 2 and re-write it, this time focusing only on your strengths and what you learned from the experience. Read it aloud to yourself.

~ I was excited to learn how to ride on my own. I like trying new things to see what I can learn about myself. I did well in the class, and decided to buy a bike. I listened to others and forgot to listen to my own gut, which is usually a good guide for me. I need to remember to consult it when I am making important decisions. I had a lot of fun on the bike, but quickly learned it was not the best choice for me as a new rider. I was willing to admit my mistake, and sold it to a more experienced rider. I chose to ride as a passenger a while longer before purchasing a more appropriate bike for my skills, knowing I would most likely need to buy a new one later. I was really proud of myself for learning a new skill and making the right decisions for me in the long run.

What, if anything, do you notice when you hear this version of the story?

What, if anything, is helpful from this version of the story? How might you see yourself or tell this story differently in the future?

Exercise 10: The Words We Choose

In addition to the stories we tell, we frequently use language and labels that may actually be reinforcing our fears and our limitations:

~ *I'm a timid rider, so I need to have a calm, reliable horse.*

~ *I'm accident-prone, so it's no surprise I got injured on that last run.*

~ *I hate playing the ninth hole; that water hazard gets me every time.*

~ *I'm really good at practice, but I lose focus when the game is on the line. My nerves take over and I can't concentrate.*

~ *I hate working out but I like the results.*

Write down some of the words and phrases you use to describe yourself and your experiences as an athlete, paying particular attention to those that have negative connotations. Notice phrases that have a 'but' in them, such as 'I'm really good on the fairways but I struggle with my short game,' or 'I play really well when the weather's decent but hate going out when it's raining.'

Look over your list. What do you notice? As you read each word or phrase aloud, how does your mind and body react? Are the words helping you feel good about yourself and how you play, or are they holding you back in some fashion?

Research has shown that constantly repeating the same thing causes us to continually re-learn that same thing. As you look at this exercise, are these words and phrases you want to be re-learning? Can you imagine words or phrases that might be more constructive to be repeating and reinforcing? For example, compare 'I'm really good on the fairways but I struggle with my short game' with 'I'm really confident on the fairways and I'm focusing on improving my short game.' What do you notice when you read the second sentence?

Return to your list, and rewrite the words and phrases into forward moving statements, ones that are encouraging your progress and where you want to be going rather than reinforcing beliefs about your struggles. This is different than creating positive affirmations; it's noticing the impact of the language you are using and modifying it to be helpful versus harmful.

~ *I listen to my gut when I ride, and I enjoy a horse that fits me well.*

~ *I pay attention to and take good care of my body. When I have an injury, I take the time to heal and recover.*

~ *The ninth hole is a challenge for me, and I am going to keep playing it until I figure out the puzzle.*

~ *I'm working on my mental focus, learning how to stay in the moment in games as well as practices.*

~ *I'm willing to workout because it gets me the results I want.*

Exercise 11: Sport Specific Loss Inventory

In addition to our stories, we often have losses associated with our lives, and many of those losses are related to our sport. Looking at our losses can often help us understand where some of our mental blocks started, and can help us assess if they need to be addressed in the present in order to improve our current performance.

Sometimes we stay stuck in our lives unless we look directly at the ways we've been wounded and we grieve. This is an exercise that allows you to acknowledge what you have loved and lost, the hurts, disappointments, endings, and betrayals you have endured. In validating your losses, you begin the grieving process. In this exercise, I am asking you to consider specifically losses or hurts related to sports, athletics, or your passions but it is also common to have other losses come up and find that they may have had an unexpected impact in your athletic journey.

In writing your inventory, consider the following:

What are the losses you've endured that stand out to you from earliest memory to the present? Are any of those losses tied to sports, athletics, or your passions? What has made you sad, what has broken your heart, what has left a gap in your life, what do good-byes bring up for you? If, as you engage in this exercise, any of the losses feel as painful today as they did when they occurred, it might be helpful to talk with a professional to help resolve any lingering emotions.

There is no right or wrong way to do this. Simply let your heart speak to you as you review the losses you have experienced. Be gentle with yourself as you complete this inventory, and contact your friends, family, or your coach for support if needed.

~ One of the earliest painful memories was when I played in my first softball tournament and my father promised to come to the game. I kept looking for him in the stands but he never showed up. I later found out he didn't want to upset his girlfriend's plans and so he never told her about my game.

~ When I think of a 'gap in my life' growing up, the biggest one was a sense that I never quite measured up to my dad's expectations. No matter how hard I played, no matter how many trophies I won, he always seemed to think I could do better.

~ I moved around so much when I was little that I never felt that sense of belonging, of being part of a team. I always wanted to stay in one school long enough to make friends and work my way to the top.

~ My parents' divorced when I was nine. My dad had been the one to get me into riding, but he had to move to a different state for his job and could only watch me ride when he was able to come to town on rare occasions. I missed having him be a part of something that had been so important to us.

~ I had ACL surgery during my junior year of high school. I was one of the best players on my soccer team, playing Premier and loving every minute of it, and suddenly I was out, couldn't play for such a long time. I watched everyone move on, getting better, while I spent my time in physical therapy. I felt left out, lonely, and unimportant.

~ My sister was the star equestrian in our family. Everyone loved watching her ride. I always felt I could never be as good as her. I was so competitive with her that I missed being friends with her. Now she lives across the country and I hardly get to see her. I wish I knew her better.

~ My aunt died when I was twelve. She was my biggest cheerleader, coming to every game, every sport I played. All my friends loved her. It was such a shock when she was diagnosed with cancer and died so quickly. Games never felt quite the same after that. I always thought of her and missed her so much.

~ We lost the state championship in my senior year. We were favored to win but we collapsed under the pressure. I hated ending my high school career with that.

~ I was kept late at school and had to rush to the field to join my teammates for the game. I didn't get to warm up as much as I needed to, and I put pressure on myself to prove I deserved to play when the coach put me in. I was so focused on being perfect I didn't see the other player coming across the field until we collided, breaking my ankle when he fell on my leg. Now when I play I'm more worried about getting hurt again.

~ I had a minor fall not long after I returned to riding following the birth of my daughter. Normally I would have jumped up, dusted myself off, and hopped back on. Instead, I felt myself shaking and unsettled. I sat on the ground until my trainer came over to see if I was hurt. I wasn't even bruised, but ever since then I've been terrified of falling and getting hurt.

What did you discover? Were there any surprises?

Exercise 12: Learning From Loss

Losses or endings typically bring new beginnings or ways or being. Often, but not always, it helps to look at what was gained as a result of the loss. This type of perspective takes time and each grief journey is unique. If you feel ready to do so, spend a few moments writing about what has resulted from each loss: what you may have learned about yourself, your strengths, and your values.

~ *I learned my father was human, that he had flaws like the rest of us. I was disappointed in some of his choices, and they hurt me, but I also learned that I wanted to make different choices for my own life. If I made plans with a friend, I wanted to honor them even if something better came up. If someone wanted me to choose him over someone else I also cared about, I learned to speak up about my values. If he continued to insist, I realized it wasn't a good relationship for me and let it go. I forgave my father for his weaknesses while choosing a different path for myself.*

~ *I understood the value of hard work when I tore my ACL. I missed being part of the team, but as I recovered, I found other interests and friends. My life broadened beyond just soccer, which helped me when I went to college and no longer played. I pursued recreational, intramural games for fun, and found competitive outlets in many areas of my life. It was painful when I was a teenager, but as I got older I had a much better perspective and realized my world didn't end with the injury; it simply opened new doors for me.*

~ *My aunt's death was extremely painful, and it took a long time to be able to do things that reminded me of her without hurting. One day I realized I was holding on to her loss so tightly that I was forgetting all our good times. That turned it around for me; I began thinking about all she had taught me, and I started to do things to honor her. I found my joy in sports again. Now I imagine her cheering me on no matter what I am doing.*

~ *I learned I could survive loss; that life does go on despite not wanting it to for a long time. I found I had more strength than I knew, that I could dig deeper than I thought. I learned I could hurt deeply and I'm no longer afraid of strong emotions. I feel more joy since I am also able to feel more pain.*

~ When I look back at my injuries, I can see a pattern for most of them: I was too rushed, unfocused, not present. I didn't take time to get centered, and on a few occasions I didn't listen to my gut. If I had, I probably would have made a different choice. The accidents weren't really as 'out of the blue' as I thought.

~ I realized the birth of my daughter changed my willingness to take crazy risks. Suddenly I was responsible for the life of another being, and I wanted to be around to take care of her. My priorities shifted. I still want to ride, I still want to have fun, but for now, I'm not willing to be as daring as I was before starting a family. Perhaps when she's older I will feel differently but for now this feels like the right decision.

What have you learned about yourself? In what ways might this awareness be helpful for you now?

~

The stories we tell ourselves often focus on the negative aspects of our experiences. The language we use to describe ourselves, and the significant events in our lives, hypnotizes us into believing the stories are true, and only the version we remember is correct. In reality, there are many perspectives and many truths.

In the above exercises you have looked at your experiences from different angles, hopefully gaining some new perspectives in the process. It is now time for many of the stories to be put away, no longer useful or relevant. While they can't be erased, they can be relegated to the attic.

Exercise 13: Scrapbooks

Look at all the stories you have written, your loss inventory, and any other memories that continue to interfere with your current participation in sport. Close your eyes and imagine creating a scrapbook. See the cover, and give it a title, such as 'Old Memories' or 'No Longer Helpful Stories'; whatever fits for you. Open the book, and imagine putting all your stories onto the pages. Add photographs, newspaper articles, things others have said to you; whatever you associate with your memories.

Take one last look at the pages before closing the scrapbook. Now imagine wrapping it in white tissue paper, and setting it inside a brown cardboard box. Making sure your book is protected, close the box and tape down the flaps. Visualize carrying it up to an attic, down into a basement, or any similar storage space that contains other old memories and souvenirs. Find a place for the box on a shelf, inside an old trunk, or just in a corner of the room. Set the box down, and say goodbye, knowing, like many old souvenirs, it will soon be forgotten. Yet it is still there, and someday you may come back and find it, surprised at the discovery of this old relic. It has simply faded from memory, no longer needing to be sitting in your living room as a coffee table book you insist upon showing to everyone who comes over. It's part of the past, a distant story. Close the door on your storage space, return to the present, and open your eyes.

What did you notice? What was it like to put the memories into the scrapbook? Was it helpful to know you didn't need to destroy the box, that it was still in the storage?

Exercise 14: Statement of Strengths

Write a list of the strengths you have discovered about yourself in the exercises in this chapter. Put them into statement form, something that is easy for you to remember and say to yourself.

~ I have a strong gut and value listening to it. I am willing to try new things, and when I fail I'm willing to admit it and move on. I can feel deeply, both painful and joyful feelings. I am able to forgive others and make good decisions based on my values. I am able to step back and gain perspective on things, and grow from what I learn.

~ I work really hard and I practice the skills I need to improve my game and my life. I listen well to instructions. I am courteous and encouraging to others. I accept my defeats graciously while maintaining a strong desire to push myself to win.

~ I am highly motivated. I will practice in all kinds of weather and adverse conditions as long as it is safe. I appreciate the support I receive from others and give back when I am able. I can tolerate being uncomfortable. I am good at solving complex problems and keeping my focus on my goals.

~ I'm clear about my values. My family comes first at this point in my life. I will find a way to balance my need for excitement with my commitment to be present for my children. I chose this and I feel good about my choice.

Exercise 15: Flexible Stories

Reviewing your Vision Statement and your Statement of Strengths, write a new story about yourself. This story should reflect how you want to be as an athlete, what you bring to your sport, and how you want others to see you.

~ *I am a full participant in my life. I push myself to see what I am capable of while being a good teammate to others. I demonstrate leadership and kindness, being a good example in all that I do. Winning reflects the hard work I put in, and losing challenges me to learn more about myself. I am good at solving complex problems and staying focused. My goals align with and support my values. Others see me as congruent: my words and actions match.*

~ *I run for the sheer joy of it and plan to run as long as I am alive. I take the long view so I can stay fit. I am self-motivated and run in all conditions as long as it is safe. I can be uncomfortable and still run. I listen to my coach when I need advice. I value encouraging others to share in my passion, and I volunteer teaching children to become lifelong runners. I run for my own satisfaction.*

~ *I love being a mom, a partner, and a competitive rider. I am willing to struggle to find the balance between the important aspects of my life, knowing it will never be perfect. I will listen to my heart and make decisions from that place. I hope to instill my joy and passion of riding in my children, and if it is not their passion, I will support them in finding their own.*

Is the story you are now telling different? Is it a more flexible story, one that might be motivating for you?

The greater the ability to experience flexibility in how stories are told and to let go of stories once they no longer have positive value, the greater the ability to adapt to new circumstances and experience. Continue to notice when unhelpful stories become stuck in your mind. If that occurs, repeat exercises 7, 8, 9, and 13 in this chapter to see if putting those stories into your scrapbook frees you up to pay more attention to your strengths and values.

CHAPTER 4

THE CHATTERING MIND

Our brains are quite busy, thoughts running through them constantly. Most of the time we don't notice what they're saying because we're focused on the task we are doing. However, when we are stressed, anxious or fearful, our brains often go into overdrive, and it's easy to believe what they're telling us is the truth.

We often view our thoughts as real, rather than simply as words wandering through our minds. For some reason negative thoughts that scare us, judge us, or remind us of painful events often 'stick' more than other random ones that are occurring with equal frequency. We tend to scan for them, grab them, and hold on to them tightly, believing they must be true if they are always showing up. Yet in reality they are just words, holding no more power than the myriad of others that come and go without notice.

Exercise 16: Crazy Brain

Take a moment to bring up something you are afraid of, something that causes you distress or gives you fits of anxiety. It might be standing at the face of a sheer cliff while your partner waits for you to start leading the climb, serving for match point in the finals of the state championships, jumping 1.40 meters for the first time, or running a slalom course in poor conditions. Visualize it as vividly as you can. Notice what your mind is telling you.

~ *I can't do this. What if I fall? What if I don't put the protection in correctly and it fails? What if my partner thinks I'm taking too long? I should be able to do this! Stop it! What an idiot!*

~ *The game is on the line. I can't mess up. My coach is expecting me to win. My dad will yell if I screw it up. I can't believe I had to go into a tie-break; I should have put this away when I could. I always fall apart under pressure. Everyone thinks I can't do this.*

~ *The jump looks enormous! There's no way I can do this! What if my horse refuses? What if we knock a rail? What if I fall off? FOCUS!*

~ *I used to be able to do this! What's wrong with me? Why can't I do it now?*

Where did your mind take you? What did you notice as the thoughts came into your head? Did some stick more than others? What happened to your visualization when they did stick?

Exercise 17: Step Away From the Thought

Choose one of the thoughts from your visualization, perhaps one that feels familiar, negative, and powerful. Take a moment and repeat it a few times while imagining the words to be true.

~ *I'm going to fall and I'm going to get hurt just like last time.*

What did you notice? How did it feel to say those words and imagine them to be true?

Now repeat the same thought, but this time start with "I am thinking the thought that…"

~ *I am thinking the thought that I'm going to fall and I'm going to get hurt like last time.*

What did you notice when you said it this way? Was there a difference?

Now repeat the thought one more time, this time adding, "I notice I'm thinking the thought that…"

~ *I notice I'm thinking the thought that I'm going to fall and I'm going to get hurt like last time.*

What happened this time? Did the words have the same impact as the first time you said them? What, if anything, is different?

Exercise 18: Don't Think About a Yellow Duck

What just popped into your mind when you read the above exercise title? For most, it was a yellow duck, probably the little rubber ducks you've seen as baby bath toys. I'd like you to sit for a few moments and erase the image from your mind. Whatever you do, don't think of, picture, or even say the words yellow duck.

What happened? Were you able to clear your mind? If so, how did you know you weren't thinking of a yellow duck? Did you think of something else only to come back to the yellow duck? What are you noticing every time the words are repeated?

Getting into a tug of war with our thoughts, trying to get them to stop, actually only increases the attention we pay to them. Research repeatedly demonstrates that attempting to suppress thoughts actually results in increasing their frequency. Defusing or detaching from thoughts allows them to pass, freeing energy to put our attention where we want it. 'We go where we look' applies not only to physical movement but mental focus as well. If we are continually looking at the negative, fearful, or judgmental thoughts our minds will be negative, fearful, and judgmental. Learning to hold such thoughts lightly, rather than hoping they stop happening, is the secret to loosening their grip.

Exercise 19: Holding Thoughts Lightly

Write down negative, fearful, or judgmental thoughts you frequently say inside your head or aloud to others. Be creative, allowing yourself to play with some of the following techniques to see which ones allow you to detach from their power:

~ Imagine a skywriting plane flying overhead, pulling a banner with the thoughts attached. See it move farther and farther away, the words becoming smaller and smaller.

~ Imagine the plane billowing the words out behind it as it writes them in puffy white smoke. Change the color. Make it glittery. Gently float them apart until they evaporate into the sky.

~ Sing the thoughts. Imagine them coming out of your car radio. Use different genres of music: rap, country, opera, and different singers, male and female. Vary the volume, turning it up and down repeatedly. Slow it down until it is barely intelligible, then speed it up until it sounds like gibberish.

~ Picture a comic character sitting on a table in front of you. Imagine the character speaking the thoughts in its voice, fully animated and adamant about what it's saying.

~ Visualize a chorus line dancing to your thoughts, synchronizing their steps to the words.

~ Imagine your negative, fearful, or judgmental brain as a separate being. Label it: *crazy brain, Fred, Chatty Cathy.* When the thoughts pop in, simply remind yourself, '*Oh, that's just Fred, no need to pay him much heed.*'

The purpose of this exercise is to find a way for you to move thoughts from being held tightly in your fist to opening your hand and having them sit lightly in your palm where you can look at them rather than through them. From here, it's easier to gain perspective; from here they can be carried off by a gentle breeze.

CHAPTER 5

BECOMING COMFORTABLE
WITH THE UNCOMFORTABLE

~ I hate the feeling I get when I get anxious. My stomach hurts, my mind races, my head hurts. I just want it to stop and then I'll be able to focus.

~ I start riding and I'm fine, but then my horse shies at a sound and my gut seizes up. I feel panicky and avoid that part of the arena.

~ I fell on that run and haven't skied on it since then. Every time I go up the lift I tell myself I'll go on it but when I get off the chair I feel so freaked out I make up a reason to stay on the ones I'm more comfortable with.

~ I usually do well. I expect to win. My coaches expect me to win. I want to get to the Olympics and I hate losing. Sometimes I put so much pressure on myself I almost throw up before I compete.

~ If only this feeling would go away everything would be fine. When I'm feeling better I'll do what scares me. If I lose, I'm a failure.

Familiar sentiments? The problem isn't with having those, or other, similar thoughts. The problem arises with the behavior associated with the thoughts. In each instance above, *avoidance* is the common theme.

Exercise 20: What Are You Avoiding?

Think back on a time when you felt anxious and talked yourself out of doing something. Perhaps you needed to go for your long run and you worried you might not be able to go the whole time or at the pace you wanted. You look out the window and it's raining. *'It's okay, I'll just do the long run tomorrow when the weather should be better.'* Perhaps your coach wants to move you to the 4.0 tennis team and you're afraid you won't be able to play as well as the others. *'I think I need a bit more time on the 3.5 level. The coach just wants me there to fill the spot. He thinks I'm better than I am.'*

Write down what you came up with, including your thoughts and rationales. Take a moment and re-read what you wrote. Create a list of the sensations you were feeling, both then and now as you remember the event. *A pit in my stomach; my hands were sweating; my heart was racing.*

Looking at the thoughts, feelings, and actions, write down what it was you didn't want to experience.

~ *heart racing*

~ *failing, losing*

~ *looking stupid, being embarrassed*

~ *falling, getting hurt*

~ *the jerking in my hands, the yips*

~ *disappointing my partner, coach, parents*

Going back through your list, make a note about what you fear might happen if any of the above was to occur.

~ I might have a heart attack; I might faint and fall off my horse; people might see the panic in my face and think I don't belong on the team.

~ Losing means I'm not good enough; my parents will be disappointed in me; my teammates will stop talking to me and being my friend; my coach will promote someone else and not want to work with me anymore; it'll prove my old trainer was right: I don't have what it takes.

~ Everyone is coming to watch me play, they'll laugh if I lose; I'm not as afraid of losing as I am of making a stupid mistake and looking like an idiot; it will mean I'm not as good as I thought I was; my parents won't keep paying for my lessons if I don't keep improving; my friends will tease me if I screw up.

~ If I get hurt my parents won't let me compete anymore; I might get seriously hurt and not be able to work anymore; I've been hurt before, never badly, but maybe the next time it will be serious; I might be hurt so badly I'll never be able to ride again; I'm older now and it takes so much longer to heal; if I wreck my knee one more time I won't be able to go to the junior trials.

~ My coach has so much faith in me, if I lose he'll be crushed; my mom always told me I could make it to the Olympics and I don't want to let her down, it's always been her dream; my husband has shouldered most of the load at home with the kids that if I don't finish with a qualifying time it will seem unfair that he's given up so much.

Look at each of your fears. First, objectively, how likely are they to occur? If they might happen 10 percent of the time, then they aren't likely to occur 90 percent of the time. Yet notice how natural it is to focus on the part of the equation that is scariest. Logical reasoning, while helpful for assessing risk, isn't as helpful for managing fear and anxiety. Neither is avoidance.

As you review your list of fears, themes may emerge, such as the fear of being hurt, being rejected, and being unlovable. Unfortunately, there are no guarantees that those fears may not be realized at some point in your life and your participation in a sport. The question is not, 'How do I make sure I don't get hurt or disappoint someone,' the question is, 'Am I willing to accept that I may get hurt or disappoint someone, and do it anyway?'

Life involves risk, and most sports increase that risk. We will lose, be embarrassed, make mistakes, fall down, forget simple things at key moments, and feel afraid. We may push ourselves only to have something out of our control—such as an injury—crush our dream. In some sports the risks of injury and death are higher; in others the potential to lose and let ourselves, or others, down is greater. The irony is that if sports could be made mistake proof, injury proof, and loss proof, they would also lose their enjoyment, challenge, and interest. It is the balance of pushing oneself against a foe, whether that foe is oneself, an opponent, or the elements, and seeing if on any given day we can come out victorious where most of us find the pleasure in participating. What if you could feel all your fears and do it anyway? What if, instead of hoping they would disappear, you accept that they will tag along with you?

Exercise 21: Willing or Not?

Look at your list, and one by one ask yourself:

~ Are you willing to accept that this activity has risk and you cannot protect yourself from every element that may cause you injury?

~ Are you willing to lose, and sit with the disappointment of your coach, parents, teammates, friends and still see yourself as a worthy person?

~ Are you willing to push yourself to try new challenges, knowing you will probably look awkward, stupid, and will make mistakes as you keep growing?

~ Are you willing to work hard? To put forth the amount of effort required striving for your dream? To believe in yourself even if others doubt?

~ Are you willing to let your fears ride with you rather than spending all your energy trying to keep them away from you, which keeps your focus on the fear instead of what you need to be doing in the moment?

I am not suggesting any of these feelings are pleasant or desirable; I am merely acknowledging the reality that they will most likely show up with far more frequency that we'd like. It is our attempts to *avoid* them that give them power and divert our attention to what might go wrong that is the real problem. If, instead, you are willing to *accept* that uncomfortable feelings will occur, you will have an easier time focusing on the tasks at hand.

Exercise 22: Where Are You Looking?

Write your fears on an index card, using one card per fear. Flapping the cards at eye level in your non-dominant hand, stand in front of your bathroom mirror and brush your teeth. Be as annoying with the cards as you can be.

What did you notice? How challenging was it to keep your hand flapping? How much energy did it take? How focused were you able to be on the task of brushing your teeth?

Next, tape the index cards on the mirror, in various locations, including near, but not directly in your line of sight. Repeat the exercise of brushing your teeth (your dentist will be thrilled).

Was there any difference? What impact did the cards have on brushing your teeth? Was your attention drawn to them, and if so, what happened next? Was it easier to bring your attention back to the task? How much energy did it take compared to the previous exercise?

Instead of trying to 'get rid of' or 'argue with' or 'push through' your fears, what might it be like if you allowed them to be present, and when you noticed yourself being drawn to them, you were able to bring your attention back to the task at hand? How might this be helpful dealing with fears and anxieties when you are participating in your sport?

Exercise 23: Tagging Along

Remove the index cards from the mirror and hold them in your hand. Take a few minutes to look at the words on each card, one at a time. Sit for a few moments and notice the thoughts, feelings, and sensations emerge as you contemplate each card. Continue to notice, without judgment, observing:

~ *Where did the feeling start?*

~ *Can you move it from one spot to another?*

~*Can you change the strength of the feeling?*

~ *Does the intensity of the sensation increase or decrease as you sit with it?*

~ *What color is the feeling?*

~*Can you adjust the intensity of the color? Change it to another color?*

What happened? Did your relationship to the feelings and sensations change? Did the power of the emotions diminish? Sometimes the sensations come in waves, and if you allow yourself to merely observe the motion of the wave, rather than fighting it, it passes quickly. How might this awareness be helpful for you?

~

Next time you engage in your sport, I invite you to carry the cards with you, literally or figuratively, as a reminder that they don't need to disappear. Imagine your fears riding in front of you in the saddle, or place them in the pocket of your shirt. Picture them along the sidelines of the soccer field on a bench with your teammates, their chatter blending in with the cheers of the crowd.

If your mind drifts to the words on the cards, simple say 'thank you mind' and return your attention to the task at hand. Rather than focusing your attention on trying to make them go away, it's much easier to let them simply be while focusing on what you have already defined as important: your values and vision.

CHAPTER 6:

BEING PRESENT

~ *Be in the moment.*

~ *Come on! Get in the zone!*

~ *Focus!*

~*Stop thinking so much!*

How many times have you heard that advice? Has it improved your ability to pay attention and focus? If so, keep doing whatever you are already doing since it appears to be working for you. However, for most people, the advice to be in the moment, get in the zone, focus, or any other variation produces anxiety and frustration: *"What, exactly, am I supposed to do to be in the moment? How do I get in the zone? And I'm trying to focus!!"*

Everyone agrees performers do better when they are in the present moment and focused. The challenge is understanding how to get there. I imagine wishing, hoping, positive self-talk, and beating oneself up haven't proven to be particularly successful. Practice, and the correct practice, can increase your likelihood of success.

Exercise 24: Brushing Your Teeth

There are many things you do without thinking, having done them for most of your life. Brushing your teeth is one of them. For the next week, practice being mindful of the experience. Notice the feel of the toothbrush in your hand, the squeezing of the toothpaste out of the tube onto the brush. Pay attention as you wet the paste and begin brushing. Notice the feel of the brush on your teeth, the taste of the paste, how often you need to stop and rinse your mouth.

Your mind will wander, repeatedly. Just notice, and bring your attention back to the task at hand. Practice every single time you brush your teeth, and track if you are able to increase your ability to stay on task mentally, catching your mind when it wanders, and bringing it back gently to the act of brushing.

Exercise 25: You Go Where You Look

Imagine riding a bicycle on a narrow trail alongside a river. You can sense anxiety that something might cause you to slip and fall down the embankment and into the water. Trying to keep your fear at bay, you keep glancing at the side of the trail, telling yourself you'll be fine, the trail is wide enough, stop worrying. But before you have a chance to realize what's happening, your worst fear materializes: you're covered head to toe in dirty water and your bike is floating downstream.

What just happened?

In most sports there is a saying 'you go where you look.' Your body will naturally follow where your eyes are leading. In the above example, your fear of the water kept it in focus, and your eyes naturally followed your chatter. As your eyes fixated on what you were trying to avoid, your body went exactly where you were looking: the water.

Every sport has specific tasks associated with it; there is always something to do. Close your eyes and walk through a scenario involving your sport. Visualize the atmosphere, the people around you, what you are about to do, and what you're expecting to have happen. As you see yourself, increase the intensity of the scene by increasing what's at stake.

~ *You're stepping up to the tee on the eighteenth hole, and if you make par you'll win the championship. If you can just hit past the bunker on the left you will set yourself up perfectly for the green.*

~ *You're riding up the chairlift for your first race of the day: the slalom, which is your most challenging course. Whatever you do, don't catch an edge!*

~ *You're standing at the free-throw line and if you make the basket the team will pull ahead for the first time in the game. Come on! Focus! Don't screw it up!*

~ It's your first time back on the field after you tore your ACL; the doctors have said you are good to go, your coach believes in your ability to play, but you're scared you might get hurt, that your knee may not be quite strong enough despite what they are telling you. You can feel yourself holding back from your normal, pre-injury level of play.

Notice where your attention goes. Are your eyes focusing on the bunker, hoping your shot misses it? Reminding yourself to get it together so your skis don't snag a pole and pull you off course? The rim of the basket, praying the ball doesn't bounce off it? Playing to avoid being hurt?

If your attention is focused on what you don't want to happen, guess what? You've just increased the odds of it occurring.

So, where should you be looking?

Exercise 26: What's Your Job?

Return to your imagery of your sport; however, this time focus on the task you want to accomplish rather than on what you want to avoid. What concrete actions are necessary for you to do in order to achieve that result?

~ *I want to have a clean round, therefore as I enter the ring I will look at the first jump, keeping my eyes up and looking past it to the next one; I will silently count strides; and I will collect my horse after each jump and get him lined up for the next one.*

~ *I want to shoot par on this hole. I will focus on my targets; first the flat spot about 130 yards ahead on the right, then I will line up my next shot*

~ *I want to have a quick time on this run, skiing aggressively within my abilities. As I ride up the chairlift, I will replay the course in my mind, going over my strategy for attacking it turn by turn*

~ *I expect the ball to go in, and I will focus on the spot just above the net exactly where I want the ball to go*

~ *I am keeping an eye on the forward, making sure I know where she is at all times in relation to the ball. I am moving in rhythm with her, looking for my opportunity to steal the ball*

In each example by focusing on the task to accomplish instead of the action to avoid, your eyes are looking where you want them to go.

Exercise 27: Focus Words

In sports you must be in your body and the experience as much possible when participating or competing. Overthinking takes you back to being a beginner, when you needed to think through everything you were learning and doing. While mentally processing is useful when first attempting a new skill, it can interfere once that skill has been mastered. Trusting in procedural, or body memory, is critical to good performance.

Cueing, or focus words, can be useful for getting out of your head and reminding you to bring your attention back to the task at hand. These words don't require thought and are repeated in training to form what are referred to as 'anchors': quick, automatic reminders to do what our bodies already know how to do.

~ a runner competing in a marathon might say 'one step at a time' for the beginning, 'just do it' during the middle, and 'you can rest when you're dead' for the surge at the end.

~ a rider may use a word such as 'forward' as a cue to pay attention to how he or she is sitting, which will trigger a quick correction if necessary.

~ a golfer might repeat 'next' after each shot to remember to focus attention on the next shot and let go of the one just hit

During the next few weeks, come up with a few key words or phrases that quickly summarize important aspects of your performance. Experiment to see which words fit and which words bring you back into the moment. Incorporate them into your daily practice, reinforcing their power to assist you when you need them in an actual performance.

Exercise 28: Mindfulness Practice

Identify areas of your sport where you can practice being mindful on a regular basis. Every opportunity to practice trains you, and your mind, to more quickly recognize when you have disconnected, and trains you to gently return to the present moment. For example, grooming your horse, getting dressed for a run, putting on the practice green, waxing your skis; the list goes on. For the next week, practice being fully present while you are engaging in the activity. Recognize when your mind will wander, and gently bring it back to the task when that happens.

Continue to identify areas where you can practice being more mindful: your pre-shot routine; swimming laps in the pool; spin class; driving your car; washing dishes; engaging in a conversation with a friend.

Meditation is often recommended as a mindfulness practice. Many athletes struggle with the concept of sitting still and simply focusing on breathing. Many find greater success with more active forms of meditation, such as walking or running. Exploring different styles and finding what works best for you is the key. I encourage you to investigate meditation to see if you find it helpful in addition to the exercises above.

CHAPTER 7:

WHEN IT ALL FALLS APART

Regular practice of mindfulness, in whatever forms you find helpful, will improve your ability to focus and remain in the present moment. However, it can become a challenge to do so when things go wrong. Unfortunately, in sports and in life, things will go wrong. Rather than hoping you will never make a mistake, or will always play perfectly, it is more useful to practice recovering when it all falls apart. I once heard someone say he wanted to teach his child 'predicament training,' and the phrase stuck with me. Planning for the unplanned and the unexpected reduces the surprise when strange things occur, and strengthens our ability to be flexible in recovering when they do. Building mental resilience as a skill is as important as learning to hit a curve ball, keep a good line on a downhill run, or count strides between jumps on a Grand Prix course.

Exercise 29: Regrouping and Refocusing

List several times when you have 'lost it' while engaging in your sport, times when you were distracted, anxious, impatient, or otherwise performing far below your normal level. As you write your list, notice any judgments, criticisms, or negative thoughts that arise. See if you can merely observe these thoughts or feelings, holding them lightly without needing to make them stop.

Next, write down anything you did at the time to refocus your energy, bringing you back into the moment. Was there anything you found helpful?

If you weren't able to refocus your energy at the time, can you imagine something that might be useful based on the exercises you have already completed?

~ *I hooked a shot into the woods. I got so mad I nearly threw my club in after it. Usually when I blow a shot like that I stay so angry the rest of my game deteriorates. Somehow I remembered something a fellow player had shared and I tried it: I took a deep breath, looked up at the treetops, and reminded myself I was outside on a gorgeous day. Ever since then, whenever I mess up I do the same thing. It calms me down and lets me refocus.*

~ *I fell several times on my motorcycle when I was first learning to ride. The falls were mostly when I was coming to a stop, at very low speed. I wasn't hurt, but I was embarrassed and started to feel frightened whenever I got near the bike. A friend told me to 'look where you're going and keep your eyes up.' Now, whenever I am coming to a stop I say the words 'eyes up, straight' to remind me where to look. It helps give me something to do rather than focusing on what not to do.*

~ I was playing a tennis match for my team. We had to win our match if our team was going to be promoted to the next level. Everyone expected my partner and me to easily defeat the other players, but for some reason I was half a step off the entire first set and we lost. I kept putting pressure on myself to pull it together, which only made my playing worse. Finally, I took a few deep breaths, and repeated the words, 'move your feet, watch the ball,' and did just that. I let go of the score and kept bringing my attention back to watching the ball and keeping my feet loose. Before long we were back in the match and pulled out a victory from the jaws of defeat.

Exercise 30: Coming Back From the Abyss

The more flexibility you have in responding to the unplanned and unwanted, the easier it will be to quickly regain focus and return to the level of play you desire. Anything that brings you back into the immediate moment will help you regroup when things go wrong. During the next few weeks as you engage in your sport, notice what connects you to the present: the breathing of your horse as it canters around the arena; the feel of the grip in your hand as you adjust it to go up to bat; the crunch of the snow under your skis as you come off the lift; the feel of your feet hitting the dirt as you run down a trail. There may be one thing that jumps out at you or there may be several. Create a list.

How might you incorporate this list into your routine? Can you imagine it bringing you back into the present moment when you are frustrated, anxious, tired, or embarrassed? The more options you have available for coming back when things go wrong and the more you practice them in everyday play, the greater the trust you will have that they will be available to you when you really need them.

Exercise 31: Perspective

Look at your list of disastrous outings, those times when you lost it, when at the moment it felt like the worst possible experience, the most embarrassing, or most painful. Imagine saying to yourself: how will I feel about this in ten minutes, ten days, and ten years? If it's been ten years since an event, has your perspective changed from when it first occurred? Has that perspective been helpful? What if you could have asked yourself the ten-ten-ten question at the time it first happened? Would it have been helpful in putting the event into perspective more rapidly, for bringing you back into the moment and letting go of thoughts and feelings that might be keeping you stuck?

Again, looking at your list, bring up your mission statement. When you compare these experiences against your core values, what do you notice? How might recollecting your personal philosophy or remembering your values be of service to you when you are having a rough outing?

Here are some suggestions to bring you back into the present when things have gone terribly, horribly wrong:

~ What's your job? What do you need to be doing right now?

~ Stand quietly, wiggling your toes, feeling them flex against the ground

~ Listen to your horse's breathing as he canters; count strides

~ Look at your line on the downhill run

~ Feel the seams on the football

~ Trace the outline of the service box with your eyes before serving

~ Notice your breathing as you run; feel your footfalls; look at your surroundings

~ Repeat focus words ('forward,' 'eyes up,' 'target')

~ Repeat your mission statement: remind yourself why you are here

~ Take a moment and trace the outline of something in your immediate line of sight

~ 5-5-5: Name 5 things you can see, 5 things you can hear, 5 things you can physically touch

(I see the net, the lines on the court, the strings on my racket, the can of balls on the bench, the laces on my shoes; I hear the breathing of the woman on the court next to us, the bounce of the ball on the court, the ping as it hits her racket, the chatter from the people on the sidelines, the voice of the pro on the far court giving a lesson; I feel the tape on my grip in my hand, the fuzz of the ball in my other hand, my toes as they move in my shoe, the warmth of the sun on my back, the slight breeze blowing against my legs)

~ 10-10-10: If you're going to laugh about it later, can you go ahead and laugh about it now?

~

I was given a copy of a research paper that studied Olympic level athletes and resilience. What struck me was not that these high level competitors had been extremely focused and dedicated to their sport, which they all had been. It was that they all had something disastrous happen along the way that caused them to re-assess their values and their commitment to their sport. It was in that process that they became stronger, more focused, and more willing to deal with their fears.

Whether being cut from the team at the last minute and having to re-earn a spot four years later, or being injured and missing a key competition in addition to facing the fear of never being fully functional again, these athletes used their experiences to become even more dedicated to the hard work and mental focus to succeed. By tackling their fears, failures, losses, and injuries head on, they found strength to not only survive, but to thrive.

CHAPTER 8:

PUTTING IT ALL TOGETHER

Now that you have a vision statement, your old stories are neatly stashed away in storage, you've sat with and faced some of your fears, and you've been developing the ability to bring yourself back into the present, what's next? Creating an action plan based on goals that support your vision.

There are typically two types of goals: process and outcome.

Outcome goals are based on the outcome of an event:

~ *I will win 8 out of ten matches this season, and will move from the 3.5 level to the 4.0 level by fall.*

~ *I will qualify for the Boston Marathon by shaving 10 minutes off my best time.*

~ *I will win the Club Championship.*

~ *I will beat my best friend in the 5k run this weekend.*

Process goals focus on the how:

~ *I will practice two hours each week on my serve and groundstrokes, and arrange to play a match each week with a higher-level player to improve my game.*

~ *I will increase my interval training and speed work and keep track of my time on my long runs. I will work with my trainer on ways to shave time off my PR.*

~ *I will bring my best game to the starting tee and practice my focus words to remind myself to stay in the moment.*

~ I will focus on running my best race this weekend, and I'm willing to push myself hard to see if I can beat my best friend for the first time.

Outcome goals have value: believing in your ability to achieve an outcome can be a powerful motivator when times are tough, and having a strong desire to achieve a specific outcome can challenge you to continually improve your performance. Being able to imagine playing on the 4.0 team, running through Boston for the first time, or standing on the podium as your teammates applaud your victory are inspiring goals.

However, over-focusing on outcomes often takes you out of the moment and can set you up for frustration and failure when either it appears they are unattainable or something unexpected occurs. Recovery can be more difficult when things go wrong as judgments and criticisms take hold.

Process goals keep your attention on the task at hand, trusting that the outcome will take care of itself. Setting realistic desired outcomes, and backing them up with clear process steps, creates a template for action.

Exercise 32: Setting goals

Write down your outcome goals: your dreams, your best-case scenarios, your fantasies related to your sport. Give yourself permission to be playful and imaginative, and also to be realistic; there's no need for self-censuring at this stage.

Review your list and pull out the outcomes that you'd really like to achieve. Rank them in order of importance and evaluate them against your vision statement and your values.

Under each outcome goal, create process goals: what will help you achieve your desired accomplishment. Be specific, breaking your goals into manageable, concrete action steps.

~ *I want to qualify to run the Boston Marathon. To do that, I need to shave 10 minutes off my PR*

    ~ *I will meet with my trainer to design a program to improve my speed.*

    ~ *I will schedule an appointment this week*

    ~ *I will follow the schedule he creates and work with him as I train*

~ *I will arrange my schedule to allow me time to run regularly*

    ~ *I will block off time every morning for my workouts*

    ~ *I will arrange for my partner to be home if one of the kids gets sick so I can still run in the mornings.*

~ *I will devote time for hill runs as well as interval training*

~ *I will sign up for 2 different qualifying marathons so I have two chances to get the time I need without overtraining*

~ *I will practice my running focus cues*

    ~ *When I notice I am freaking out about time while running, I will bring my attention back to the road ahead of me and the sounds of my feet as they hit the ground. I will use those sounds to help me keep my targeted pace.*

The plan above includes the desired goal of running Boston, with concrete steps to maximize the chances of accomplishing the goal. While no one can guarantee the outcome of running in the needed time to qualify for the race, the process goals set the stage for success. Weather, injuries, a family emergency, or any unknown may affect the outcome; those are events out of your control. By focusing on the process, if the unexpected does occur, the training isn't seen as a failure; it is seen as in alignment with your personal philosophy and your values of pushing yourself, willingness to risk disappointment, and staying healthy. If making the qualifying time is the only goal that matters it becomes easier to see yourself as a failure rather than a disappointment if you miss the goal.

In addition, when you focus solely on the outcome, your attention is already in the evaluation stage rather than in the moment. Often the greatest risk of losing comes when things are going really well: your mind takes you to 'If I only shoot par on the next two holes I'll break 70!' or 'I beat them 6-0 in the first set, I've got this match in the bag,' and the next thing you know you've bogied the last two holes or find yourself in a second set tie breaker, only to lose because you are so mad at yourself for blowing the match. Your mind got ahead of the action at hand.

Process goals help us stay in the moment and trust that if we do, the outcome will take care of itself. Process goals are under our control; outcome goals are not.

Once you have established your outcome and process goals, it's important to check them against your values, your willingness to experience discomfort, whether emotional or physical, and the degree of effort you are willing to make to achieve your goals. It's also critical to evaluate what resources, support, and accountability you need, what obstacles might get in your way, and your plan to deal with those obstacles. Each item in the following exercise will help you plan for your road to success.

Exercise 33: Creating your action plan

~ What is your primary goal?

~ Why does this goal matter? How does it align with your vision statement and values?

~ How much does this goal matter to you?

~ Are you willing to put in the effort it takes to achieve this goal?

~ Are you willing to risk disappointment to put yourself out there to attempt this goal?

~ How do you plan to deal with disappointments if they occur?

~ What are your intermediate goals that will move you toward your primary goal?

~ What process goals will support you achieving your desired goal?

~ What obstacles are in your way of achieving your desired goal?

~ What is your plan for overcoming the obstacles?

~ What resources do you have to help you achieve your goal?

~ What resources do you need? What is your plan for getting those resources?

~ What type of accountability do you need to help you achieve this goal?

~ How do you want to celebrate your successes along the way?

Review your plan regularly, making any necessary adjustments. Discuss your plan with your coach, trainer, or pro to make sure your training programs align. Post it where you can see it. Practice the exercises that you found helpful: the more you practice, the more easily they will stick with you.

Above all, remember your vision and live it fully.

CONCLUSION

This is a book about sports, athletics, and performance. The skills you have learned here are skills you can bring to any and all areas of your life. They are building blocks to success as you apply them daily, whether on the golf course or preparing a presentation for work, on the basketball court or having a conversation with a loved one. Being mindful, noticing self-defeating behaviors and language, creating a willingness to fully experience emotions, and recovering from missteps builds resilience. I encourage you to revisit these exercises as needed, as situations change or whenever you may need a refresher.

Feel free to modify the exercises in any way that you may find helpful for your personal practice, and to share with me anything you have learned as a result. In addition, feel free to contact me if you would like assistance in completing any of these exercises or would like to discuss personalizing them further.

Lynda@TheWinnersMind.com

www.thewinnersmind.com

REFERENCES

Many of the exercises in this book were adapted from the wealth of knowledge within the ACT community. For further information about ACT practitioners, books, and other ACT resources, go to www.contextualscience.org.

The Sport Loss Inventory was adapted, with permission, from the Loss Inventory developed by Mavis Tsai and which can be found in the book:

A Guide to Functional Analytic Psychotherapy: Awareness, Courage, Love, and Behaviorism (2008) by Mavis Tsai, Robert J. Kohlenberg, Jonathan W. Kanter, Barbara Kohlenberg, William C. Follette, Glenn M. Callaghan

Resources for finding a therapist who deals with trauma can be found through one of the following professional organizations:

~ EMDRIA: Eye Movement Desensitization and Reprocessing International Association www.emdria.org

~ ASCH: American Society for Clinical Hypnosis www.asch.net

27202562R00049

Made in the USA
Middletown, DE
13 December 2015